Great
Hispanics
of Our Time

Roberto Clemente: Baseball Hall of Famer

Maritza Romero

The Rosen Publishing Group's
PowerKids Press™
New York

Published in 1997 by The Rosen Publishing Group, Inc.
29 East 21st Street, New York, NY 10010

First Edition

Book Design: Danielle Primiceri

Photo Credits: Cover, pp. 12, 16 (both insets) © Hy Peskin/FPG International; pp. 4, 8 (both insets),11 © Archive Photos; pp. 7, 8, 15, 19 (both photos); p. 16 © Pittsburgh Black Heritage/FPG International; 20 © AP/Wide World Photos.

Romero, Maritza.
    Roberto Clemente : Baseball Hall of Famer / Maritza Romero.
       p.   cm. — (Great Hispanics of Our Time)
    Summary: A brief summary of the Hall of Fame player known for his humanitarian efforts as well as for his athletic ability.
    ISBN 0-8239-5083-2
    1. Clemente, Roberto, 1934–1972—Juvenile literature. 2. Baseball players—United States—Biography—Juvenile literature. 3. Puerto Ricans—United States—Biography—Juvenile literature.
4. Pittsburgh Pirates (Baseball team)—Juvenile literature. [1. Clemente, Roberto, 1934–1972.
2. Baseball players. 3. Puerto Ricans—Biography.] I. Title. II. Series.
GV865.C439R66 1997
796.357'092—dc21   97-4231
                                                          CIP
                                                          AC

Manufactured in the United States of America

Contents

Born to Play Ball

There was nothing Roberto Clemente loved more than playing baseball. He was born on August 18, 1934, in Carolina, Puerto Rico. For as long as Roberto could remember, he played baseball with his friends. He practiced pitching by throwing a rubber ball against a wall in his room. When he listened to baseball games on the radio, he squeezed the ball with his hand to make his throwing arm stronger. Roberto knew that he was born to play baseball.

◀ Roberto's dream was to play baseball. Some people believe he was one of the greatest baseball players in history.

Roberto Just Wanted to Play

Roberto's father helped run a sugar **plantation** (plan-TAY-shun). He worked very hard. He taught his children to work hard too. Roberto had many jobs when he was young. One of these was to deliver milk before he went to school. His father told him that if he worked hard, he would have a good life. Roberto did as he was told, but he never stopped thinking of baseball. He didn't dream of being a star. He just wanted to play ball.

Roberto's father worked hard on a sugar plantation very much like this one in Puerto Rico. ▶

High School Sports

When Roberto was in high school, he joined the track team. He discovered that he could run fast. He was voted Most Valuable Player, or MVP, on his track team. He threw the **javelin** (JAV-lin) and learned that he was able to throw it 195 feet. He also learned that he could jump six feet into the air. Roberto played shortstop on the school's baseball team. He made the All-Star team three times in a row. He could play any **position** (poh-ZIH-shun) on the team.

Roberto was a great athlete. He could play many sports. But his favorite, and the one he was the best at, was baseball.

The Pros

Roberto was seventeen when he was asked to play on the Santurce Cangrejeros. This was a **professional** (pro-FESH-un-ul) baseball team in Puerto Rico. He played for them for three years, until 1953. Then the Brooklyn Dodgers learned of Roberto's high batting average of .356. That year, the Dodgers offered him $10,000 to play for them. That was the most money the Dodgers had ever offered a Hispanic player. Roberto joined the Dodgers in 1954.

Roberto played for a total of three professional baseball teams. ▶

A Hard Time

The Dodgers wanted to keep Roberto's **skills** (SKILZ) a secret from other teams who might want him to play for them. They sent him to a **minor league** (MY-ner LEEG) team in Canada. It was a hard time for Roberto. When he played well, they took him out of the game. When he played poorly, they kept him in the game. He was also lonely. In those days, he spoke only Spanish, so he couldn't talk to the other players who spoke English. But Roberto did not give up.

◀ The Dodgers tried to hide Roberto's talent from other teams. But another team, the Pirates, found out about him anyway.

13

Not a Star Yet

One day, someone from the Pittsburgh Pirates saw Roberto play. The Pirates had finished in last place in 1954, so they were allowed to pick new players first in the **draft** (DRAFT). They chose Roberto. In his first five seasons, Roberto was a good player, but he was not a star. In 1960, the Pirates won the World Series championship game. During that season, Roberto batted .314, hit 16 home runs, and batted in 94 runs. The five-foot, eleven-inch, 175-pound man was soon to be a hero.

It took five seasons to do it, but Roberto helped the last-place Pirates win the World Series in 1960. ▶

Most Valuable Player

Roberto's fans loved him. He could leap into the air, catch a ball, and throw it while he was still in the air. Between 1961 and 1965, he set new **records** (REH-kerdz) in baseball. In 1965, he hit 29 home runs and batted in 119 runs. That year, he was named MVP and Outstanding Player of the Year. The next year, he set a new record for having the best batting average in the league over an eight-year period.

Many people believed that Roberto was a good person as well as a great player. In 1967, he was given a "Man of the Year" award by a local group in Pittsburgh.

The Best Player Ever

Roberto was always in pain when he played ball. He had been in a car **accident** (AK-sih-dent) in 1954. He had hurt his back. By 1969, he thought he should **retire** (ree-TYR) because his back hurt worse than ever. Then he hurt his shoulder. But he stayed in the game and set new records. In 1971, the Pirates won the World Series again. And Roberto was voted MVP again. In fact, some people believed he was the best player ever. In 1972, he had a total of 3,000 hits. Only ten other baseball players had ever done that.

Playing baseball well was important to Roberto. He gave all he could to the sport he loved. ▶

Helping Others

When Roberto wasn't playing baseball, he lived in Puerto Rico with his wife and three sons. He thought a lot about helping other people. On December 31, 1972, he gathered **supplies** (suh-PLYZ) to help the people of Nicaragua. A terrible earthquake had hit their country. He boarded the airplane with some other people to take the supplies to Nicaragua. But the plane crashed into the sea. Everyone on the plane died, including Roberto.

◄ Roberto's wife, Vera, and his three sons, Richie, Luis, and Roberto, Jr., were very important to Roberto.

In the Hall of Fame

Roberto was only 38 years old when he died. Three months later, he became the first Hispanic player voted into the Baseball Hall of Fame. Roberto once said that he would like to be remembered as the type of player who had given all he could. He was a hero to the people of Puerto Rico, the United States, and to baseball fans everywhere. Today, there is a **statue** (STA-chew) of him at the Three Rivers Stadium, home of the Pittsburgh Pirates.

Glossary

accident (AK-sih-dent) Something harmful or unlucky that happens when you don't expect it.

draft (DRAFT) A time during which professional teams take turns choosing new players from colleges, high schools, and other countries.

javelin (JAV-lin) A light spear thrown by hand.

minor league (MY-ner LEEG) Lower-level professional baseball team.

plantation (plan-TAY-shun) A large farm.

position (poh-ZIH-shun) A player's job on the field during games.

professional (pro-FESH-un-ul) A person who is paid to do something.

record (REH-kerd) The top score ever.

retire (ree-TYR) To stop playing or working.

skill (SKIL) Something a person can do well.

statue (STA-chew) An image of a person or thing in metal, wood, stone, or clay.

supplies (suh-PLYZ) The food, medicine, and equipment needed for a group of people to survive.

Index